Boxe Française
SAVATE
Martial Art of France

PHILIP REED & RICHARD MUGGERIDGE

PAUL H. CROMPTON LTD.

**102 Felsham Road, Putney,
London SW15 1DQ, England**

1st Edition 1975
Reprinted 1995

© 1984
Philip Reed and Richard Muggeridge
ISBN No 0 901764 74 4

London: Paul H. Crompton Ltd.
102 Felsham Road, Putney, London SW15 1DQ

New York: Talman Company
131 Spring Street, New York, N.Y. 10012, U.S.A.

Printed and bound in England
by Caric Press,
Clerwood, Corunna Main,
Andover, Hants SP10 1JE
(01264) 354887

Boxe Française Savate,
Martial Art of France
by Philip Reed and Richard Muggeridge

Photographs by John Bristow
additional photographs by Colin Hassel

We would like to express our thanks to the people who have helped us in the preparation of this book, in particular to Charlie Howes, Gant d'Argent and British International, Richard Howes and Alan Moody, who appear in the photographs. For information about the history of boxe française in France we are deeply indebted to Monsieur Bernard Plasait, Gant d'Or and former Champion of France, who has also allowed us to select from his outstanding collection of historical engravings. His own book, Défense et illustration de la boxe française (Sedirep 1971) is the definitive work on the sport. Messieurs Jean Pierre Le Blon and Hervé Bruandet have combined top-class instruction with the great hospitality shown to British fighters in France, and closer to home, Mr. Burt Hayter has given us every assistance at Guildford's Civic Hall. Finally our particular thanks go to Monsieur Bob Alix, Directeur Technique National of the Féderation Francaise de Boxe Francaise-Savate et Disciplines Assimilées, pictured here in the salle at Vincennes, for his encouragement and advice. For any shortcomings remaining in our book, hopefully few, we alone are to blame.

boxe française

WHAT IS FRENCH BOXING?

If asked to name a characteristic French sport the average Briton is likely to think of either boules or cycling; relatively few people in this country except followers of judo and karate are aware of the popularity these Japanese combat sports enjoy in France, and fewer still are familiar with the French style of boxing, la boxe française, which uses the feet as well as fists. Yet this is a truly French sport with origins in two older kicking styles, savate and chausson, which are part of French national tradition and culture and bear the same resemblance to boxe française as the prize fighting of our 18th and 19th centuries does to modern boxing (or la boxe anglaise, to distinguish our version just using the fists).

French boxing today combines the style of punching evolved in English boxing with the kicking techniques of savate. The skills taught and the fitness and confidence which come with practice can be highly effective in personal self-defence; all the same it remains a sport first and foremost with emphasis laid on the sporting values expressed in its moral code. The fitness, agility and balance needed to deal out, sustain and avoid blows are only achieved by making efforts in training which call on unsuspected reserves of energy and determination, and just as important, teach how to recognise and respect the efforts of others. It may seem strange on the face of it to describe relations between opponents aiming to punch and kick each other as friendly, but although a contest may be hard fought the will to win is directed into scoring against an opponent within an agreed set of rules, countering his moves with superior techniques and tactics and letting him spend his energy to no effect.
The boxers (or tireurs, to use the French term) compete in a spirit of mutual respect, and win or lose, the opponent is a friend with whom the contest is shared — a fact recognised in the salute given at the start and finish of a bout.

Contests take place on three levels, assaut, pré-combat and combat: in the Combat blows are delivered at full power and a decision may be on points or by 'hors combat' where one fighter is unable to continue. Pré-combat is similar except that the system of scoring points differs and shin-pads and casques (head-guards) are worn, whereas the Assaut is judged purely on technical skill and the force behind all blows limited so that both boxers can make progress without risk of injury or being put 'hors combat'. Like karate or judo French boxing has defined grades, distinguished by colours worn on the wrist band of the glove or gant. The first grades are awarded by a club coach according to the length of the pupil's experience and the techniques learned; only when all the techniques have been covered are pupils eligible to take part in the pré-combat and combat and to take the competitive grades, the gant de bronze and the five degrees of the gant d'argent (silver). The grades gant vermeil and gant d'or are honorary titles awarded for services to the sport.

Another rather paradoxical benefit of French boxing is in its value as a form of relaxation, demanding though it is — the concentration it takes puts thoughts of any problems aside for a while and it really gives a chance to 'let off steam'.

Comparison with English boxing is almost inevitable — contests to decide the merits of the two have occurred from time to time since the 19th century, though the value of any bout where the opponents compete by different rules must be questionable. Each has its adherents, but the two are not so much rivals as 'variations on the same theme', the individual choosing whichever may be most to his (or indeed her) taste. The participation of women and girls in French boxing tends

to come as one of the biggest surprises to those only used to the English style, but there is no greater barrier to this than exists in karate. Physiological differences dictate that in women's contests no actual contact is made, to avoid the danger of injury from body blows particularly, but female players still benefit from the fitness, graceful poise and potentially useful skills to be gained for their own enjoyment and protection.

I hope that this introduction to the rules and techniques of boxe française or savate as it is still called will stimulate interest here in Britain and compensate for the way it has been overlooked so consistently in favour of its British counterpart. Students of both boxing and karate will find it a challenging and appealing extension to their skills, increasingly popular again in France and now a sport with growing international status — since 1970 a European championship has been organised and representatives now come from Belgium, Italy, Germany and Holland. It would seem that in these countries at least French boxing is starting to find the place it deserves in modern sport as the leading European martial art.

BREVET DE BOXE ET DE CHAUSSON

To trace the beginnings of French boxing we have to look back to the end of the 18th century when French sailors are known to have adopted a specialised style of fighting using very high kicks, sometimes with a hand on the ground for balance. This may have developed from contact with martial arts in the East; certainly it is recorded to have been practised aboard ships and no doubt in brawls in the waterfront bars of ports such as Marseilles, because by the time it had spread to Paris this kicking style had become known as 'Savate Marseillaise'.

First to teach savate in Paris was Michel Casseux, a flamboyant character known as 'Pisseux' around the slums of the roughest quarters where frequent fights in the dance-halls and pot-houses enabled him to distinguish different types of kicks and develop his 'théorie de la savate'. In 1820 he opened a salle or practice gym in Courtille, and his lessons attracted a number of pupils from fashionable society including the Duke of Orléans and the artist Gavarni. Besides kicks this early form of savate involved striking open-handed blows rather than throwing punches, and it was another of his pupils, Charles Lecour, who introduced the punching style after being beaten in a bout with an English boxer, Owen Swift. Determined to master boxing technique himself Lecour came to London to take lessons from the foremost boxers of the day, and on his return to France in 1830 he opened his own salle where he taught a combination of boxing and savate under the new name, la boxe française. As street robbery was commonplace this quickly became popular and soon a number of teachers were offering lessons, often together with instruction in the use of la canne d'arme which is still taught alongside French boxing today. Official disapproval in the early days meant that these were sometimes given under the cryptic title 'adresse française' (French adroitness or skill), although Lecour's brother Hubert who gave demonstrations with him promoted 'assauts-concerts' where a display of boxe française and canne was accompanied by a programme of comic songs and ballads.

Among the fighters to come into boxe française around this time probably the most extraordinary was the larger-than-life figure of Louis Vigneron, 'the cannon man'. An enormous man of great strength and agility he was a formidable boxer and in a famous bout in 1854 defeated an English boxer named Dickson; but he was equally well-known for his exploits outside the ring. As a young man he spent some time in prison for causing the death of a friend, Charles Neveu. The two were skylarking about with a group of friends when Vigneron accidentally threw Neveu through a second-floor window; he fell into a laundry tub, broke his back and died shortly afterwards having exonerated Vigneron from all blame. Vigneron also used to perform feats of strength, and for the most spectacular, the one from which he took his name of 'homme cannon', would have a cannon weighing 305 kilos fired as it rested on his shoulder. The ball, a six-pound shot, would be caught by his pupil Alexandrini. Not surprisingly both men were eventually killed performing this stunt.

It was around this time too that a fighter appeared who more than any other was to have a lasting influence on the development of modern boxe française.

Born in 1839 Joseph Charlemont began his boxing career as a soldier, fighting the best boxers of the time including Vigneron and teaching boxe française and la canne to recruits until France's war with Prussia in 1870. In the struggle between monarchist and republican factions following the French defeat he supported the republican cause, la Commune, and when monarchist forces took Paris in a week of street fighting and massacre used his fighting skills to escape arrest and went into exile in Belgium. There he opened a highly successful boxing school in Brussels and published his first book on French boxing technique. The present-day rules are based on his methods, and his name, 'le maître Charlemont', holds a place in boxe française to compare with that of the Marquis of Queensberry in English boxing. The establishment of the Third Republic with the elections of 1877 and 1878 brought a partial amnesty to the exiled Communards and Charlemont returned to a rapturous welcome in Paris, where Alexandre Dumas was among the celebrities to come and take lessons from him. In 1887 he came to London and fought an exhibition match as part of Queen Victoria's Jubilee celebration. The Sporting Life recorded the occasion as 'A Jubilee Assault at Arms'.

'Last evening a select and aristocratic company, including Lord Aylesford, several ladies, and prominent members of the theatrical and musical profession, assembled at St. James' Hall, to witness a very excellent exhibition of boxing and various athletic exercises under the management of Mr. J. Fleming, with Jack Harper and Bob Habbijam as M.C.s. The entertainment was quite in keeping with the respective reputations of the performers, notably the veteran Jem Mace, and Lees, the champion of Australia, who gave an admirable exposition of the art without fear or favour. The feats by the St. James' Athletic members, and Fred Badon were also duly appreciated, likewise the Parisian kickers armed with gloves, both of whom created great enthusiasm and laughter. They were recalled.'

In the years leading up to the first world war boxe française was at the height of its popularity and eminent fighters of the period included Charlemont's son Charles, Victor Castéres and Georges Carpentier, champion of France in 1907 before he turned to English boxing and won his world title. English boxing was becoming established in France and even tending to eclipse boxe française by 1914, but the war and virtual loss of a generation hit the sport far harder. Despite the success of demonstrations at the 1924 Paris Olympics it only enjoyed a brief recovery before dying out almost completely under the German occupation in 1940.

The most outstanding fighter between the wars had been le comte Pierre Baruzy who won the overall French championship a remarkable eleven times; as president of the Commission de boxe française after the liberation he set out to restore French boxing to its former popularity. His efforts and those of a group of committed supporters kept the sport alive, and the resurgence of interest today both in France and abroad is the measure of their success.

Contests in boxe française take place in a boxing-style ring and the fighters compete using certain prescribed types of kicks and punches which are described in the techniques section of this book. All blows must be confined to the legitimate target areas which are:—

1. For kicks; the outsides and insides of the legs, the front and sides of the body excluding the genital area and the front and sides of the head.

2. For punches; the front and sides of the head and body above the pelvis.

The back and top of the head, throat and back are excluded from the target areas.

The aim of the contest is to put your opponent 'hors combat' either by a knockout or when he is just unable to carry on; if neither of these occurs, or if the contest is in the form of the Assaut to judge technical skill without giving the blows force, a decision is reached by a system of scoring points.

Kicks must always predominate over punches — the referee will stop the bout if the fighters are exchanging too many punches without kicking, and will see that they employ kicks when he starts it again. The system of scoring reflects this, with one point scored for a kick at low level, two for one landed at medium height and three for a kick to the head. Punches score only one point regardless of where they land, and the maximum score given for a series of punches landed between kicks is no more than two points.

As the assault is judged purely on skill there is no score for 'hors de combat' which can only happen by accident or through the negligence of one of the competitors who may be penalised or disqualified. In the Pré-combat and Combat points are also awarded for the effectiveness of blows, good tactics and defence, and to put your opponent 'hors combat' either for a count of ten seconds or on three occasions for less than ten seconds wins the contest.

A contest takes place over an agreed number of rounds or reprises, normally of 1 minute, 1 minute 30 seconds or 2 minutes' duration with 1 minute between rounds. The salute is given at the start and finish of each round, which is begun on the referee's command "Allez". The referee sees that the competitors, their seconds and the spectators respect the rules; to halt the round briefly to separate the competitors or get them clear of the ropes he will give the instruction "En garde", when they must separate and take up the garde position until he re-starts the round. At the end of a round or for a halt of longer duration he will give the command "Stop". This may be at the start of the count when one competitor is 'hors combat', to give a warning, or to allow equipment such as a glove, shoe or gumshield to be adjusted or replaced.

The equipment used for boxe française includes regulation gloves or gants of 10 to 12 ounces — these extend over the wrists in a 'manchette' protecting the wrist and lower forearm when used to block kicks. The shoes (chaussures) have soft and supple soles and uppers, and the costume worn is the one-piece tenue intégrale or 'intégrale', sometimes in club or team colours. A standard gumshield and box are always used for protection, and for training or the pré-combat a headguard (casque) and shin-pads (jambières) are added to soak up some of the punishment.

Charlemont

9

technique

Chassés

For a chassé kick bring up the knee of the striking leg to touch the chest and turn sideways so the hip is towards the opponent before making the kick. When the leg is straightened you should strike the target with the heel and sole of the foot. At the same time the opposite arm must be thrown backwards for an exchange of power. Chassés may be aimed at your opponent's legs, body or head, but the principle of raising the knee up to the chest and opposite shoulder applies in each case — this stage of the kick, called the groupé meaning bunched or concentrated stage, is what gives the blow its force. Chassé means driving out or forcing away and when aimed at an opponent's leg the kick is termed chassé bas, or low chassé.

Starting from the garde position, one leg forward and feet spaced shoulder width apart, raise the front leg to touch the chest, turning sideways by pivoting on the supporting foot, and then bring down the raised foot on your opponent's knee or thigh, throwing that counterbalancing arm back. Keep the other arm across your body for protection and bend the supporting leg so you get your whole body weight behind the kick.

To make the chassé kick to the body (chassé médian) or the head (chassé figure) the strike must be angled upwards but the movement is otherwise the same with the foot pointing sideways on impact. A chassé kick to the body is also termed a chassé d'arrêt or stopping chassé because it stops your opponent coming forward and drives him back beyond arm's length, unable to land a punch.

Top left: Jumping chassé médian; groupé, saut or jump, frappe
Top right: Chassé d'arrêt
Bottom: Chassé bas; garde, groupé and frappe or strike

The way to get within striking distance of an opponent and deliver a chassé kick before he has time to step back out of reach is to use the technique called chassé croisé, the crossed chassé.

The kick is made with the forward leg, but first bring the back leg forwards past and *behind* it so thatthe legs are briefly crossed, raising the front leg into the groupé position to make the kick. To get the maximum effect from this you should jump forward with the back leg as the front one is raised and kick as you land, still throwing out that arm for extra power. Don't signal the move by doing it in stages; practise until it is fast and fluid and return to a stable position when it is completed.

One further style of chassé exists, the forward chassé or chassé frontal. Unlike the kick already described this is delivered without turning the hips sideways-on, but the knee is still raised to the chest and the kick must be to thrust the opponent away with the sole of the foot. The so-called 'direct' or forward and upward kick with the top or point of the foot is forbidden in contests.

Top: Chassé croisé
Centre: Training with pads, chassé figure. Note that this time
the supporting leg is kept straight to give the kick extra height.
Left: Chassé frontal

Fouettés

In this type of kick you should strike your opponent with the top or point of your foot — the blow may be aimed at the head, legs or body but is always struck horizontally from the side. To do this first raise the striking leg, bent at the knee, and turn the foot you are standing on outwards to leave you sideways-on to your opponent. With the lower part of the leg held back against the thigh. This is the armé or ready position for the fouetté, and again the opposite arm is used to counterbalance the movement — this time not thrown straight back as in the chassé but swung down, back and up to help make the turn to the side. Finally you strike by straightening the knee so that the top of your foot comes round and hits your opponent on the side of the head (fouetté figure), side of the body (fouetté flanc) or the side of the leg (fouetté bas). Unlike the chassé which has the weight of your whole body behind it the fouetté has only the weight of your lower leg, so its effectiveness depends on speed and the extra tension given to the muscles that straighten the leg by turning your body to the side. Snap the knee out straight. Fouettés must always be as horizontal as possible — fouettés rising at an angle are forbidden in contests, and the impact of the strike must come from straightening the knee; to swing the whole leg sideways from the hip is illegal except in a backward turn, the revers.

Far left: Fouetté figure countered by fouetté bas.
Left: Fouetté figure and the parade or block
Above: Stages in the fouetté; garde, armé position with the knee pointing at the target, strike or frappé.

Above: Don't cross your legs after making the kick (left) or you will be vulnerable to a footsweep (centre); keep your feet spaced shoulder-width apart (right).

Below: There are two ways to reach your opponent quickly with a fouetté from a distance. One is to jump forward off your front leg, kicking with it as you land. The other is to step forward to bring the supporting leg nearer before making the kick — this technique is termed marché croisé (bottom).

Coup de pied bas, the low kick

This may be aimed at either of an opponent's legs below the knee, the front leg to stop it being used for a kick or the supporting leg to make him lose his balance. It is always carried out with the back foot as shown, dragging the foot forward as if it were a match you were striking on the floor and leaning backwards so that the sudden release from friction gives it power. Once the leg is straight it should be locked into a rigid unit with the body and swing forward as the body leans back. Bend your own supporting leg to keep the kick low and increase your reach. The blow is always delivered with the inside edge of the foot, and the arm on the same side is swung downwards and back to counterbalance. The other arm may be swung back in the same way or used to block an opponent's attack.

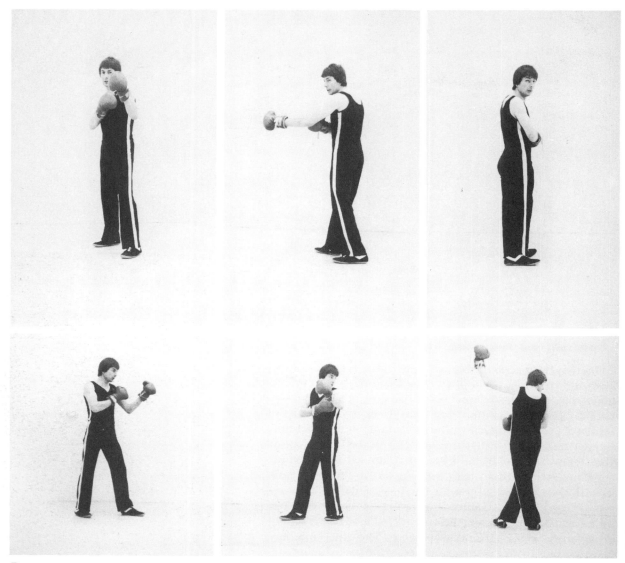

Revers

There are three kinds of revers or reverse kicks. One is the revers latéral, which is made by turning your whole body. This starts from the normal garde position with feet shoulder-width apart, left foot and left arm forward.

Without moving your feet turn your body to the right, all the way round so you end up looking at your opponent over your right shoulder. Pivot on both feet and swing your left arm round and up to help you turn. Now the right leg will be crossed over the left — lift the foot and swing it round to strike your opponent with the sole, then place it back on the floor so that you are facing him in the garde position again, this time with your right foot and right arm forward. Keep your right arm across your body to protect it as you turn.

The revers can be delivered at high level to the head, revers figure, to the body, revers médian, or to the legs, revers bas. The whole move must be executed rapidly so that you only

Left: Revers latéral
Right: Revers bas (above)
　　　Revers figure (below)

turn your back on your opponent for a moment — to lose sight of him for any longer puts you at a serious disadvantage. All the same the revers is a kick with considerable power delivered from an unexpected direction. Like the fouetté it is always dealt from the side, never upwards.

A second style of reverse kick is the revers frontal — for this the body stays facing front, but the kicking leg is crossed in front of the other, lifted and brought back across so that it strikes your opponent with the outside edge of the foot, usually at head height. The whole movement is circular and the foot must be moving sideways at the moment of impact — no upward or angled kicks are allowed.

The third revers, termed revers 'jambe tendue' (straight or outstretched leg), is made by turning sideways-on to your opponent, raising your leg straight up from the hip and bending the knee, striking him with the sole of your foot. Again the kick must be delivered horizontally and is normally aimed at the head — it is often followed immediately by a fouetté with the same leg.

Opposite page: Revers frontal
Above: Revers jambe tendue
Below: Revers bas aimed at an opponent's supporting leg while he attacks with a fouetté

Punches

Boxe française has adopted the punching techniques developed in boxing and the target areas are the same, the front and sides of the head and body above the pelvis. No punches below the waist are allowed. The referee will halt the match if too many punches are being exchanged without the use of a kick, so the way to use them is singly or in a short flurry between kicks, or in the kick-punch combinations known as enchaînments. Five different kinds of punches can be distinguished and these are described below.

Jab

Strike from the shoulder with the leading arm, usually the left because most people fight with the left leg forward. Push the arm out straight, just as you would for a press-up, and give the arm a twist at the last moment so that the knuckles are uppermost. Keep the other arm in for a guard, the glove protecting the face and elbow in to protect the body. Bring the leading arm back into the guard immediately after throwing the punch. A jab can be aimed at the head or body.

Cross

This punch is also quite straight, but with a slight twist of the hips to bring the rear arm forward, again aimed at the face or body. The twist from the hips gives the cross extra power.

Hook

This is a punch with the leading arm like the jab but sideways, round in a small arc for speed to get round an opponent's guard to the side of the head. (Jab-hook is a common sequence). Hooks are usually aimed at the head, as they don't develop much power for attacks to the body.

Swing

Swings are also sideways movement but with greater power because they are usually made with the rear arm with a twist of the body from the hip, moving the fist in a much bigger arc than for the hook. Even though it comes from the side it must always strike with the front surface of the fist, the first joints of the fingers and thumb downwards, and not with the palm of the hand.

Uppercut

The uppercut is usually driven to the body — it can be made to the head but you are lucky to land one there. It usually works after a flurry of punches, not as a leading punch, perhaps after a one-two when you've got close in. It strikes upwards, usually to the solar plexus and heart, with lots of hip movement for extra power. Often the back heel is raised off the floor as your weight goes forward. Keep reasonably up-right — don't lean right forward or you'll get kicked in the face.

It does little good to get in a hit on your opponent if you have to take two or three kicks or punches to do it. There are two ways to prevent him from hitting you — one is to evade his blows or retreat out of range, the other is to block or divert them before they land. An experienced fighter will do both these things to stop his opponent scoring points, and take advantage of his vulnerability once a blow has been blocked to launch a counter or riposte. Feet and hands can both be used to block your opponent's attacks. The chassé d'arrêt keeps him beyond arms length, while a chassé bas or coup de pied bas can be used against his leading leg to stop him raising it or bringing it forward for a kick. You can use your hands to ward off a punch or kick to the head or body — these blocks are known as parades.

Techniques for avoiding rather than blocking an opponent's blows are known as esquives and take various forms — the bob-and-weave familiar to English boxers for ducking under an opponent's punch is also used in boxe française, described as the esquive rotative because of the U-shaped movement of the head and body down and away sideways in the direction of the blow — you should bend from the knees and keep on looking at your opponent, both to anticipate his next move and to choose your own. Just bending forward from the waist is a mistake, as you cannot watch your opponent any more and your lowered head is exposed to easy kicks and uppercuts. The esquive rotative can be used to duck under high kicks too.

Opposite page
Top: Parade chassé (not to be confused with a chassé kick) against a left jab and again against a right cross — the glove and forearm are swept across to divert the punch to the side, past the head.
Below left: Parade bloquée, glove turned down with palm outwards to block a fouetté kick to the side, fouetté flanc.
Below right: Esquive rotative, ducking under a fouetté figure.

This page
Above: Esquive rotative to each side.
Below: Esquives by moving the head and body to either side.

but these may also be avoided by stepping back out of the way (esquive en rompant, or esquive by disengaging) or by leaning head and body right backwards (esquive en arrière, or backward esquive). This last may be combined with an attack on your opponent's supporting leg to unbalance him with a fouetté bas or coup de pied bas while he is making the high kick. A chassé kick to the head or body can sometimes be avoided by sidestepping as well as diverting the blow by a sideways parade, and an attack on the legs can be avoided either by taking a step backwards or simply raising your leading leg out of the way.

Opposite, top: Parade and sidestep to avoid chassé médian
Below left: Exterior sidestep as an esquive to avoid chassé médian
Below right: Esquive by lifting leg attacked with fouetté bas

Enchaînements and the importance of distancing

The techniques of boxe française, kicks, punches, esquives and parades, can all be learned individually and improved by repeated practice, but successful free fighting in practice and competition depends on more than knowledge of these techniques in isolation — they can be made far more effective by combining them into rapid sequences termed enchaînements, meaning a series of linked moves. A single punch or kick is relatively easy to block or avoid — you are more likely to score if your opponent is still reacting to your first blow when you attack him with a second and third. The first move in an enchaînement may just be a feint to deceive him and make him react in a predictable way that gives you an opening for a real blow — for example raising your forward leg as if in preparation for a fouetté to the body may lead your opponent to change his guard, ready to block the kick with both arms in the parade opposition. Instead of making the kick, change sides by jumping from one leg to the other, attacking as you do so with a fouetté to the head with the other leg. This is much more likely to connect than the pretended attack, as you have made him lower his guard to protect his other side and the changed direction of the attack is unexpected. While he is recovering from the surprise you may have the chance to hit him again, but only if your own movements are fast and fluent. If you have to stop and think what to do next you lose the advantage, and so an important part of training is working out and practising enchaînements of techniques which go together readily.

As a general rule you have to get closer to your opponent to land a puch than is necessary for an effective kick, simply because legs are longer than arms. For this reason combining kicks and punches in enchaînements requires good judgement and continual adjustments of the distance between yourself and your opponent. As well as stepping in to come close enough for a punch you may have to move back or to one side to get far enough away for an effective kick. If it is made from too close in a fouetté goes round behind your opponent and you tend to strike him with your shin instead of the top of your foot; step away to the side as you kick and you will catch him properly with your foot at longer range and so achieve much greater speed and impact. A chassé too is difficult to execute

Above: Sideways esquive to avoid a jab to the head, countering at the same time with a jab to the body and following up with a right cross and left hook to the face: an enchaînement of punches.
Below: Enchaînement of a punch with two kicks. Left jab to the face (blocked with a parade) is followed up with a chassé bas and fouetté figure.

at very close range and ineffective except as a push away — if you step back or sideways a little before raising your leg into the groupé position you can get maximum force into the blow, with the knee almost straightened as your foot connects. To follow these kicks up with a flurry of punches you would have to come in closer again for a moment. These movements in and away to put you at the right distance for your chosen technique are called déplacements, and judging them correctly makes the difference between good boxing and wasting your energy on inefficient blows. Watching the déplacements your opponent makes helps you to anticipate his attacks and work out a defence and riposte or counter of your own.

Examples to show the value of déplacement

Above: a sideways déplacement, used to move to the best distance for a fouetté kick aimed at the plexus. A sideways move in the direction your body is facing (i.e. to the right if you are in the usual garde or stance with left foot forward) is described as an interior sidestep, or déplacement intérieur.

Below: Too close to attack with a chassé from the back leg until a déplacement to the side increases the distance. A sidestep in this direction, away from the direction your body is facing, is called an exterior sidestep, or déplacement extérieur.

Déplacement before a revers latéral, a turning reverse kick. The distance between the fighters is initially suitable for a punch but too close for a kick — the first step in the turn, out to the right, is also a means of adjusting the distance to suit the kick.

Above: Enchaînement of a kick, two punches and a second kick: fouetté bas followed with jab, cross and revers frontal to the head.

Below: Attacks and ripostes. First attack (Right cross to the face) is avoided by an esquive rotative and countered with an uppercut to the body followed by a left jab to the head; these are countered in turn with a chassé frontal.

Following page: Attack and esquive followed by an enchaînement of two punches and two kicks as riposte.

Stage 1. garde

2. Attack with left jab to the face avoided by sideways esquive.

3. and 4. Riposte of uppercut to the body and left hook to the face followed by

5. déplacement by stepping to the side to get the right distance for two kicks,

6. and 7. fouetté to the plexus

8. and 9. chassé to the side.

BOXE FRANÇAISE

SAVATE

Students of boxe française are graded according to experience and level of proficiency, each grade being represented by the symbol of a glove (gant) of a particular colour. The first five grades, blue, green, red, white and yellow, may be awarded by a teacher at club level and indicate progress from basic knowledge of kicks and punches to familiarity with all the techniques of boxe française. They are known collectively as the Gants de Couleur, coloured gloves. Control of balance and movement, judgement of distancing and the ability to combine techniques into enchaînements are all developed until on reaching the Gant Jaune (Yellow glove) a student is eligible to enter contests with the aim of gaining the Gant de Bronze, first of the competitive grades, or progressing to the technique grades at higher level, the three degrees of the Gant d'Argent (Silver glove).

The following pages provide a syllabus of techniques to be mastered for each of the coloured grades. These are derived from material issued by the Fédération Francaise de Boxe Française-Savate et disciplines assimilées, the controlling body for the sport in France. Students preparing for grading work with a partner, practising the sequences of attacks and ripostes together so that each is familiar with both roles. Two sequences from each grade are illustrated here; candidates for grading would prepare all the sequences for their grade and also be asked to demonstrate in a bout of free sparring their familiarity with techniques appropriate to that grade in action.

1. GANT BLEU (BLUE)

Attacks
Illustrated: Sideways déplacement → fouetté médian with forward leg ——————
Forward déplacement by marché-croisé → chassé bas with forward leg ——————
Forward déplacement by marché-croisé → fouetté médian with forward leg ——————
Sideways déplacement → fouetté médian with back leg——————

Counters or ripostes
—————————————— *Parade opposition → marché-croisé to riposte with chassé bas*
———————————— *Esquive intérieure*
———————————— *Parade opposition*
———————————— *Parade bloquée → riposte of fouetté médian with the back leg*
(A riposte with the same technique as used by your
opponent in his initial attack is also called a remise)

Attacks
Illustrated: Chassé bas with the back leg ——————————————
Jab to the face ——————————————————————
Cross to the face —————————————————————
Coup de pied bas —————————————————————

Counters or ripostes
——————— *Sideways esquive → counter with fouetté médian*
——————— *Parade bloquée → jab to counter*
——————— *Sideways esquive of the body → counter with cross to the face*
——————— *Esquive by raising the leg attacked → riposte by fouetté médian, chassé bas or cross to the face*

2. GANT VERT (GREEN)

Attacks
Illustrated: Fouetté bas with the back leg ─────────────────
Chassé médian with the back leg ─────────────────
Revers médian with the back leg ─────────────────
Forward déplacement by marché-croisé and revers bas ─────────────────

Counters or ripostes

——————— *Esquive by changing to opposite garde (forward leg back)* → *counter with fouetté bas*
——————— *Parade chassé*
——————— *Parade en opposition*
——————— *Esquive by lifting leg attacked* → *riposte with right hook*

Attacks
Illustrated: Sideways déplacement and swing ————————————
Jab to the body ————————————
Cross to the body ————————————
Coup de pied bas ————————————
Revers tournant (turning revers kick) to the body or head ————————————

Counters or ripostes

——————————— *Esquive rotative → counter with cross to the face*
——————————— *Parade chassé with right arm → counter with left jab to the face*
——————————— *Parade bloquée with left arm → counter with right hook to the face*
——————————— *Esquive by stepping back → riposte with fouetté médian with back leg*
——————————— *Parade opposition → counter with swing*

3. GANT ROUGE (RED)

Attacks

Illustrated: Jumping fouetté figure (fouetté to the head) ——————————

Right hook to the head ——————————

Left hook to the head ——————————

Chassé médian, sauté-croisé ——————————

Chassé tournant médian (turning chassé to the body) ——————————

Revers frontal to the head ——————————

Counters or ripostes
—— *Parade bloquée en opposition → sidestep (déplacement) and counter with chassé médian with the back leg*
—— *Parade bloquée with left arm → riposte of right hook to the head*
—— *Esquive backwards → counter with jab to the head*
—— *Esquive by step to the side → riposte with chassé bas with the forward leg*
—— *Parade bloquée → riposte with left jab to the face, right cross to the body and left jab to the face*
—— *Esquive by leaning backward → riposte with fouetté with forward leg*

Attacks
Illustrated: Right hook to the body ——————————————————
Jump forward and attack with coup de pied bas ——————————
Left hook to the body ——————————————————————
Jumping fouetté médian with forward leg ————————————
Jumping chassé bas with forward leg ——————————————
Revers tournant bas ————————————————————————

Counters or ripostes

——— *Parade bloquée with left arm and sidestep intérieur → counter with left and right hooks to the head*
——— *Sidestep intérieur → riposte of revers with forward leg*
——— *Parade bloquée with right arm → counter with left and right hooks to the head*
——— *Parade bloquée with right arm → riposte with coup de pied bas*
——— *Esquive by sidestep extérieur → riposte by left jab and right cross*
——— *Esquive by a step backwards → riposte with a jumping chassé-croisé*

4. GANT BLANC (WHITE)

Attacks in enchaînements

Illustrated: Chassé tournant bas → déplacement for fouetté with the other leg → right cross to the face → left jab to the face ————

Jumping chassé with the forward leg → revers frontal to the head with the back leg → jab and cross ————

Cross and jab to the head → revers tournant → coup de pied bas ————

Jumping fouetté bas with the back leg → fouetté figure (same leg), right leg forward in change of garde and left uppercut to the body, right hook to the head ————

Counters or ripostes

————————— *Parade chassé, riposte of left jab and chassé bas with forward leg*
————————— *Sidestep, riposte with right uppercut and any kick*
————————— *Esquive by step backwards, riposte with jumping chassé bas and a punch*

————————— *Esquive rotative → riposte of right uppercut to the body and left hook to the head*

Attacks in enchaînements
Illustrated: Chassé frontal to the body → jumping fouetté figure with the other leg ——————
Revers sauté-croisé and chassé médian with the back leg ——————
Jumping fouetté bas with the forward leg → right hook to the head left uppercut ——————
Sauté-croisé coup de pied bas → jumping fouetté médian with the other leg and chassé bas with the same leg —

Counters or ripostes
– *Parade bloquée and sidestep → riposte by jab to the body*
– *Parade chassé → riposte with revers tournant bas*
– *Parades bloquées → riposte of right hook to the head → revers figure with the forward leg*
– *Esquive by taking a step backwards, changing to opposite garde → riposte of fouetté figure with the forward leg*

5. GANT JAUNE (YELLOW)

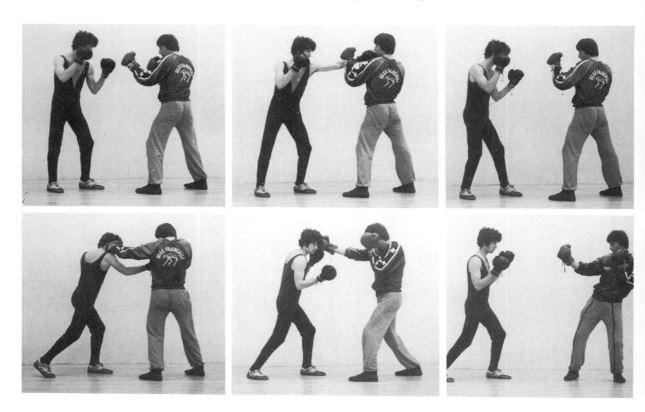

Attacks in enchaînements
Illustrated: Jab to the face → jab to the body → uppercut to the face ————————

Jumping revers figure with the back leg → chassé médian same leg → cross ————————
Chassé frontal médian with forward leg → jumping chassé médian with the other leg ————
Jab to the face and cross to the body → chassé figure with forward leg ————————

Counters or ripostes

———— *Downward block of uppercut, riposte of left and right hooks to the head → one step backwards, changing garde, fouetté bas with forward leg*

———— *Sideways esquive → riposte of left uppercut and hook, both to the head*

———— *Parade chassé → riposte of chassé bas with forward leg and swing from the right*

———— *Either an esquive or a parade → any technique in riposte*

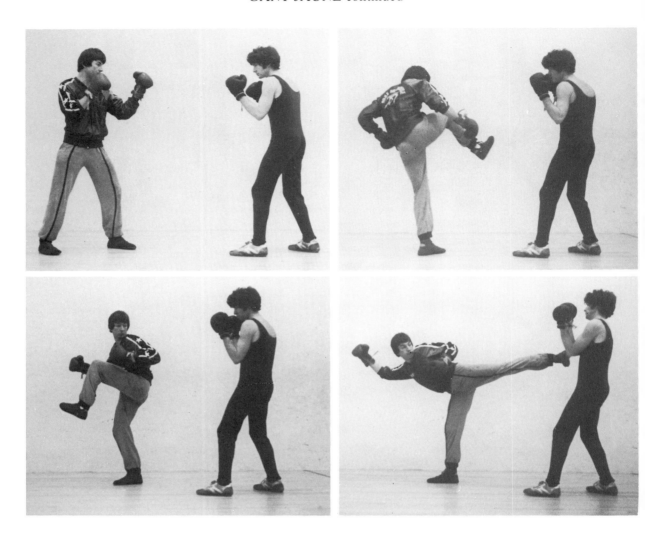

Attacks in enchaînements
Illustrated: Chassé bas with the back leg → turning chassé médian ————————————
Jumping revers figure with the forward leg → jab to the face → cross to the body → déplacement for
fouetté médian with the back leg ————————————
Jumping revers tournant → then with other leg fouetté médian and fouetté figure ————————————

Counters or ripostes
———————— *Forearm block, riposte with revers figure with the back leg*

———————— *Parade opposition → riposte of chassé frontal to the body or head with the back leg*
———————— *Parade bloquée → riposte with chassé tournant médian*

61

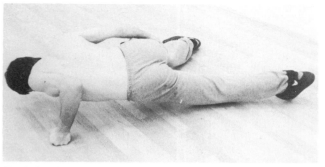

Training for boxe française

The best training for boxe française is naturally to be had from practice bouts and sparring backed up by instruction in and practice of specific techniques, but is is also possible to prepare yourself for the sport generally in a wide range of ways. Individual boxers will find the particular training régime that suits them best, but the methods suggested here are all beneficial.

Running ('footing' in France) and circuit training build up the stamina indispensible for good training and contests, and weight training develops strength. Skipping is a traditional form of boxing training which gets you used to moving around on your toes and aids fitness and co-ordination. To develop really fast reactions some fighters also practise la canne, the art of fencing with canes, which is a sport in its own right and is often taught with boxe française in France today.

Before a bout or any training session you should always take the time to warm up and do some stretching. This improves your performance and prevents pulling stiff muscles by too sudden a start. This applies particularly to the strains of high kicking, and a few ways of warming up for kicks are shown here.

Opposite page
Above: One-arm press-ups to strengthen the arms and body for punching. Warming up — spread your legs wide and touch your head to the knees
Below: La canne
This page
Above: Stretching exercises. Raise your knee to touch your chest, then outside to touch your shoulder. Repeat for both legs.
Below: Raise one knee and hold the foot back, then turn on the spot on the other foot, keeping your back straight. Turn right round in each direction.
Sideways stretching — raise your foot sideways to touch your partner's hand held at shoulder level

Punch bag and training pad work

A disadvantage of using a punch bag is that because it can't hit back you can develop an over-confident style, unconsciously leaving yourself open to counters. Bear your guard in mind all the time, bob and weave to avoid imaginary ripostes after striking the bag and stay light on your feet. Remember that kicks must be made cleanly with the feet, not with the shins, and after throwing punches quickly move back or to the side, déplacements to make distance for your kicks. It is a good idea to hang a bag low sometimes to strengthen kicks aimed at the legs.

The static nature of a punchbag is unrealistic for boxe française and an answer to this problem is to use training pads when you can train with a partner. When wearing the pads you should always keep moving, giving your partner a mobile target. Only hold up the pads when you want him to strike, which he should try to do as rapidly as possible with the agreed blow. Vary the intervals between blows and the distance to the target slightly to keep him alert, and as a further refinement you can clip him on the side of the head with one of the pads if he leaves his guard too low after striking.

If you are training alone without access to a bag, shadow-boxing is still possible, and it always forms a useful part of a warm-up. Serious shadow-boxing should be paced for a set number of rounds — if your are training for a contest of six rounds for example, shadow-box for six rounds fast and use them to find the right pace. When you go into the ring for the fight you are usually a little tired from an expenditure of nervous energy — to match this state it is a good idea to run for about half a mile before you start to shadow-box.

Le Combat — tactics and ringcraft

When you go into the ring for a contest you're there to win, to do well. Whether you do or not depends on how determined you are, how hard you've trained for skill and stamina, and a lot is going to depend on luck. But there are still plenty of points to remember that will help set the odds in your favour.

Boxe française is a very unstatic sport — when you fight you usually dance about instead of staying rooted to one spot; it makes you harder to hit. Keep on your toes and keep your feet roughly shoulder-width apart for balance as you move between kicks. Use the space available, moving in to kick or punch and moving out again quickly. The best place to be is in the centre of the ring, free to move in any direction. If your opponent manoeuvres you into a corner wait for him to come forward and sidestep out round him, turning him in instead and keeping him there with fouettés and punches from each side if he tries to do the same.

As your opponent attacks you he is vulnerable — block and counter before he can move away. When you attack hit him as hard as you can to make him worry; make him feel your power. If you tap him about he'll get confidence, just as he will if you let up and slacken the pace. Never show you're tired even if you are, make yourself try harder instead.

Concentrate on your opponent's moves all the time or you risk leaving him an opening that can lose you the fight. Keep your eyes on his chest area to have an overall view of him. Practise your techniques repeatedly, so that when you have the opportunity to use them they come as an instinctive reaction and you only need to think about them for a split second.

My own tactics tend to be to work for points rather than a knockout; one way of doing this is by making your opponent come to you and using stopping techniques, raising your front foot to block his kicks and ready to counter with chassés of your own. If you can make someone fall, kick his legs from under him, the judges will remember who went down and it can make up otherwise unequal scores.

Glossary of common terms

English equivalents are given here for the names of French boxing techniques, but for a full understanding of the techniques themselves it is best to follow the sequences of illustrations in the technique section.

Allez!	Begin!
arbitre	referee
armé	ready position before a kick
arrière	behind, backward motion
assaut	light contest in technical skill
autorisé	allowed
bas	low
balancé	leg swing
boxe	boxing
bras	arm
casque	headguard
chassé	driving or forcing away
chaussure	footwear
coin	corner
combat	full-power contest
compte	count
coquille	box
corps	body
coup	blow
coup de pied	kick
coup de pied bas	low kick
coup de poing	punch
crochet	hook
croisé	crossed
déplacement, décalage	distancing movement
direct	straight
droit	right
enceinte	ring
enchaînement	sequence of blows combination
esquive	avoiding technique
figure	face

flanc	side
fouetté	whiplash
frappe	strike
gant	glove, or with colour to indicate grade
garde	guard position
gauche	left
groupé	ready position before a kick
hanche	hip
haut, en haut	high
hors combat	unable to continue
intégrale	one-piece suit
interdit	forbidden
jambe	leg
jambière	shinpad
latéral	sideways
médian	middle
non combat	no decision where both boxers are disqualified or the match is abandoned due to spectator behaviour
parade	blocking technique
pesée	weighing
pied	foot
poing	fist
pré-combat	middle category of contest with contact and full protection
protège-dents	gumshield
règlements	rules
rencontre	match
reprise	round
revers	back kick
riposte	counter
soigneur, second	second
tenue	costume
tireur, tireuse(f)	boxer

Members of Guildford Boxe Française club who appear in this book

Charles Howes   Richard Muggeridge
Philip Reed, club coach   Richard Howes